Tyler Stoner's
Trippy Adult Coloring Book

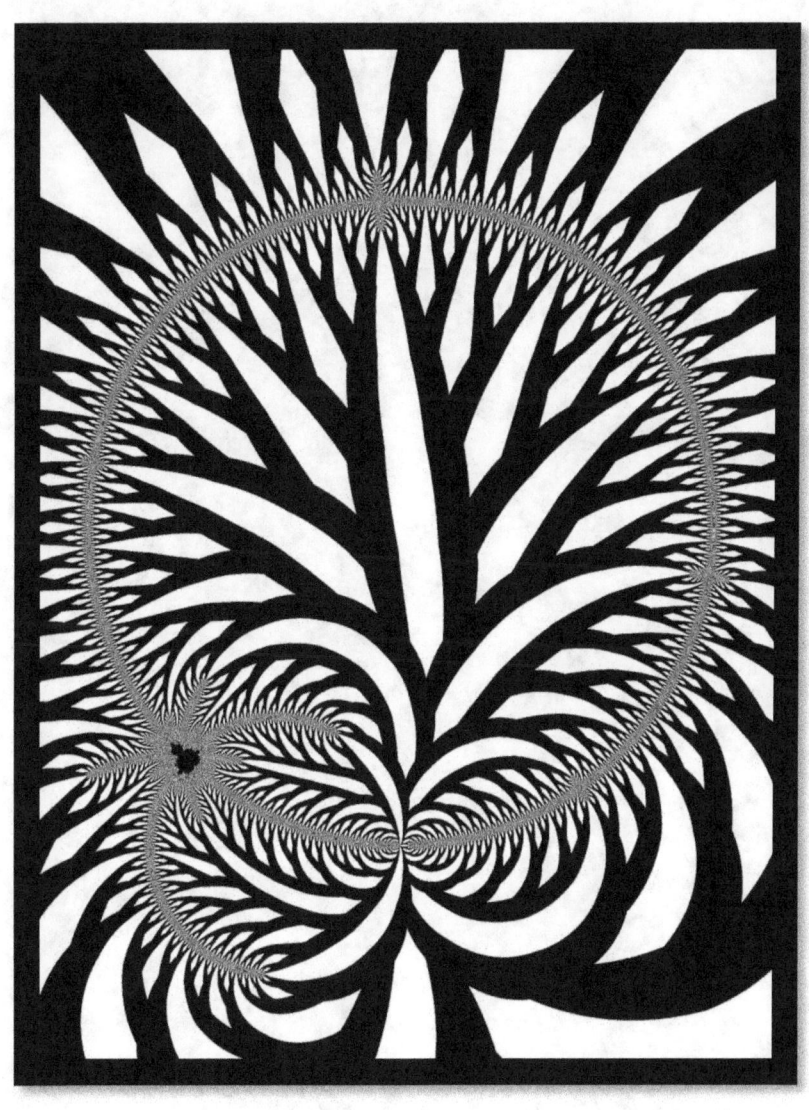

Color and Chill with 20 Far Out Designs

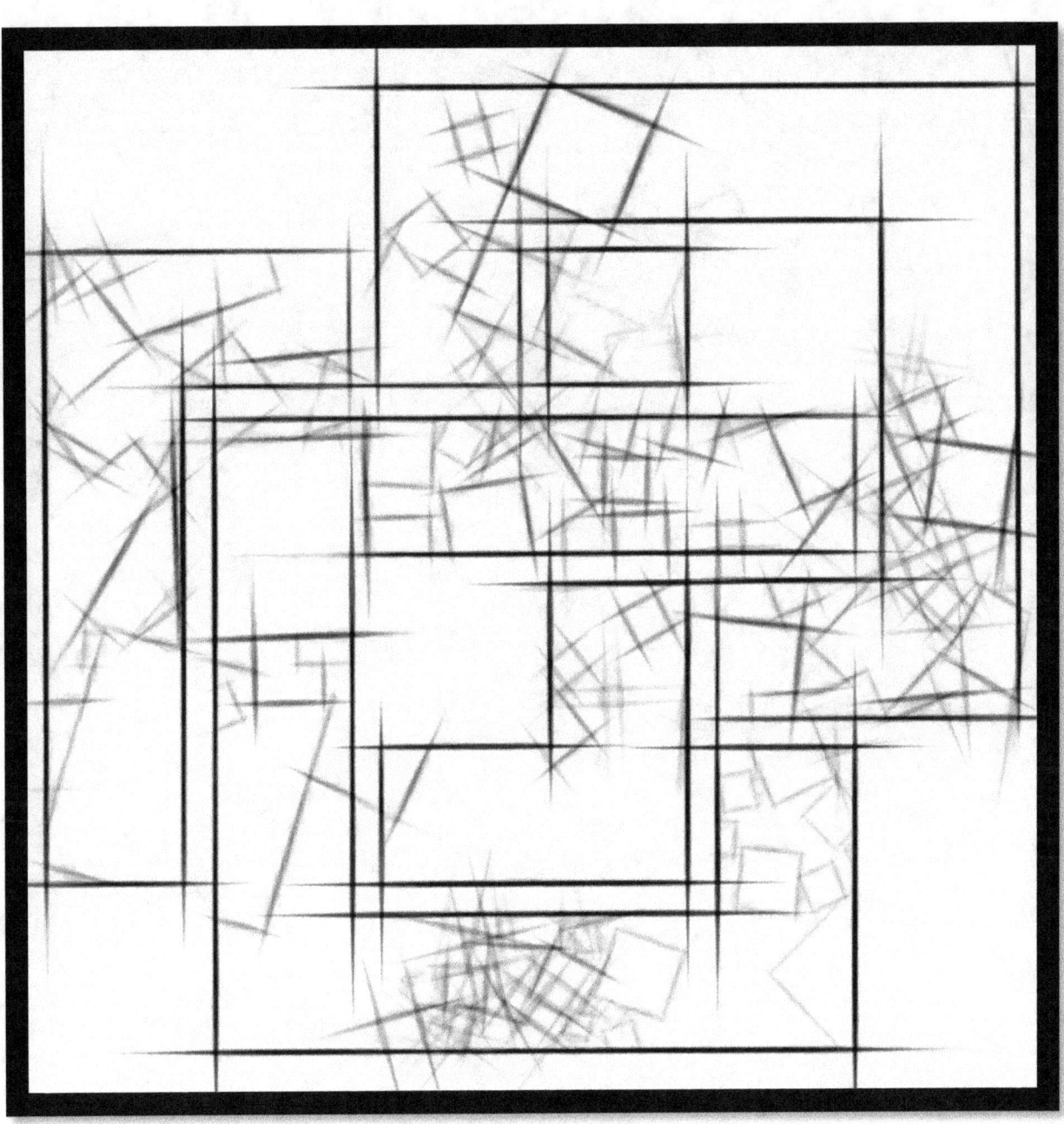

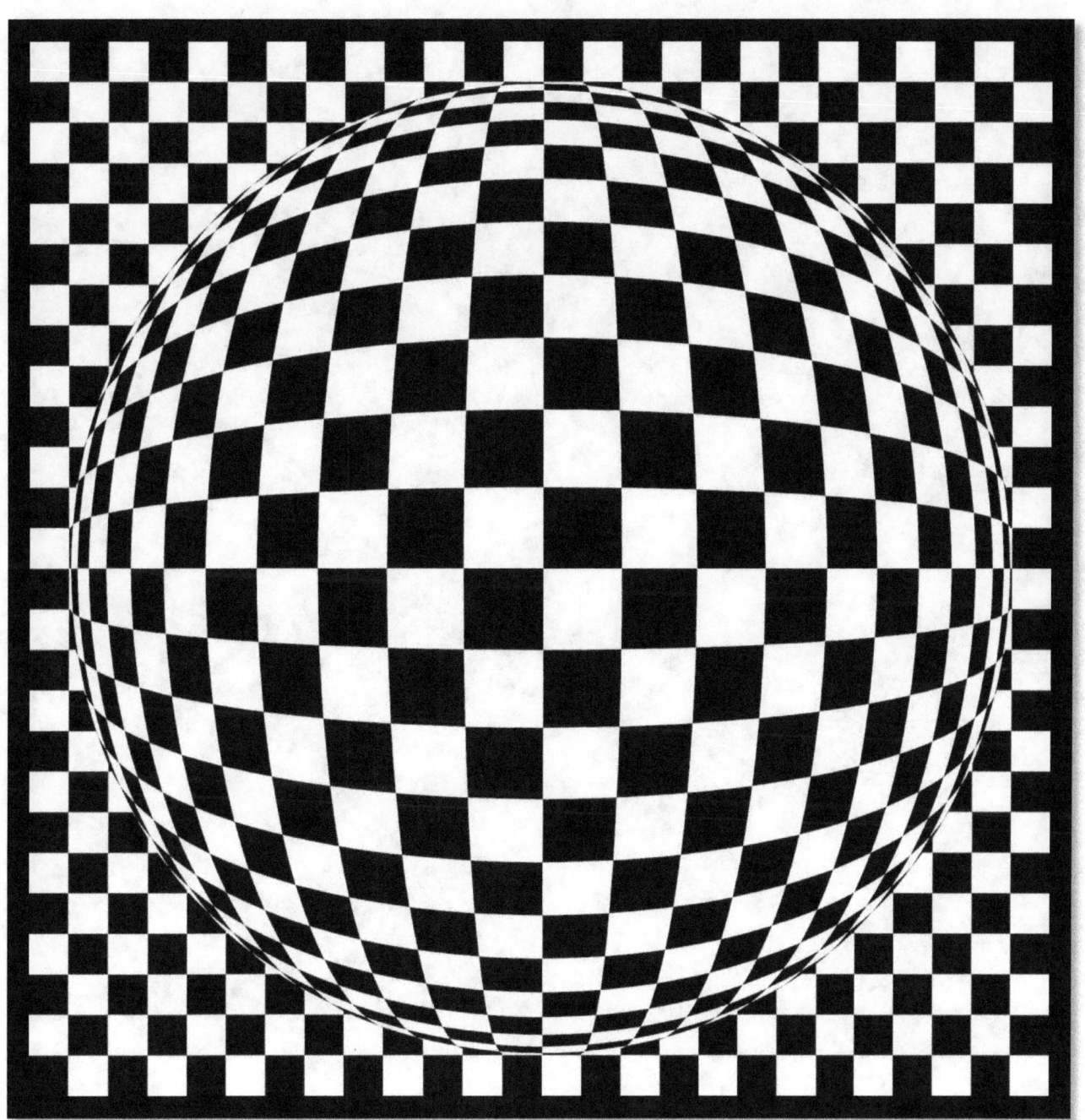

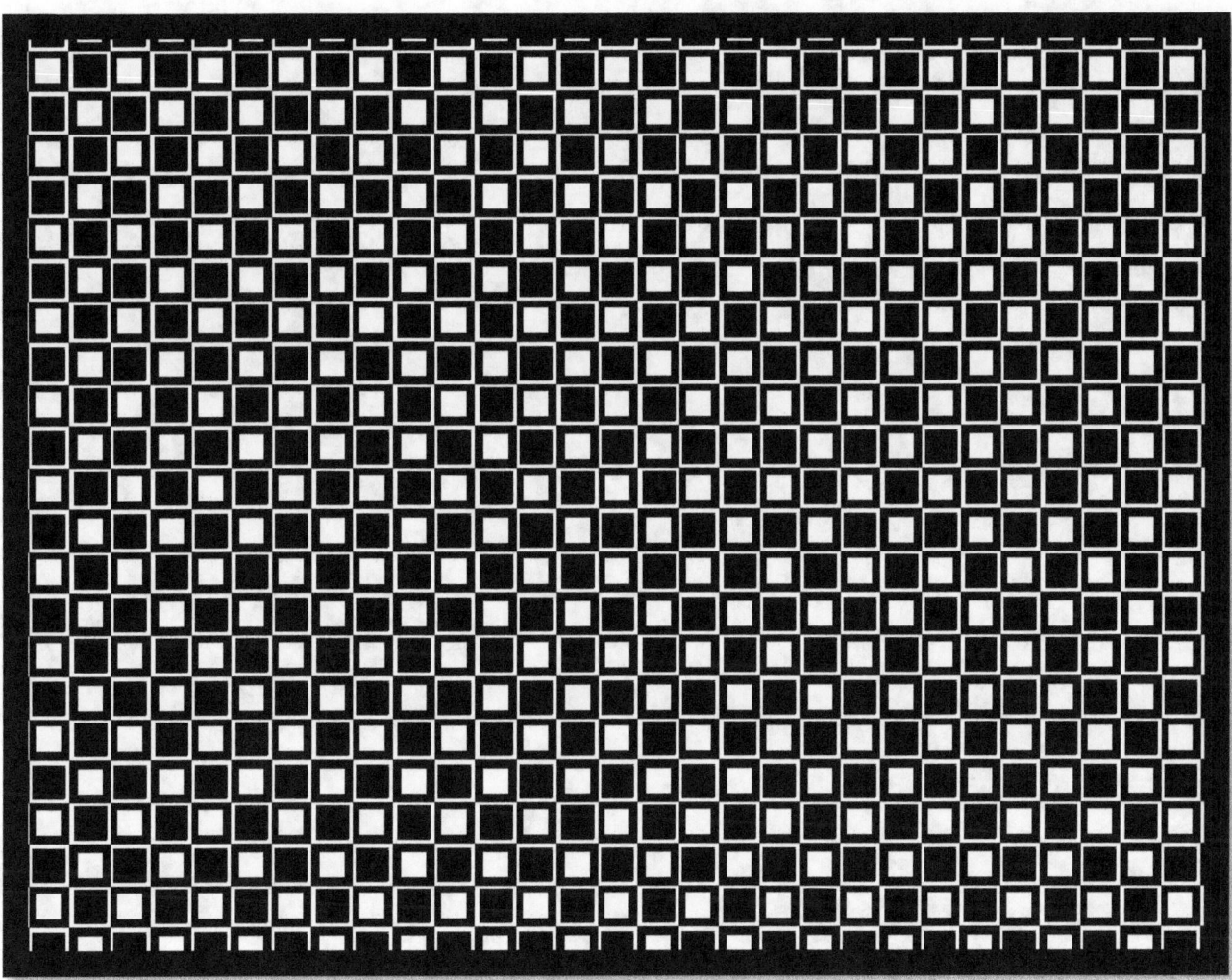

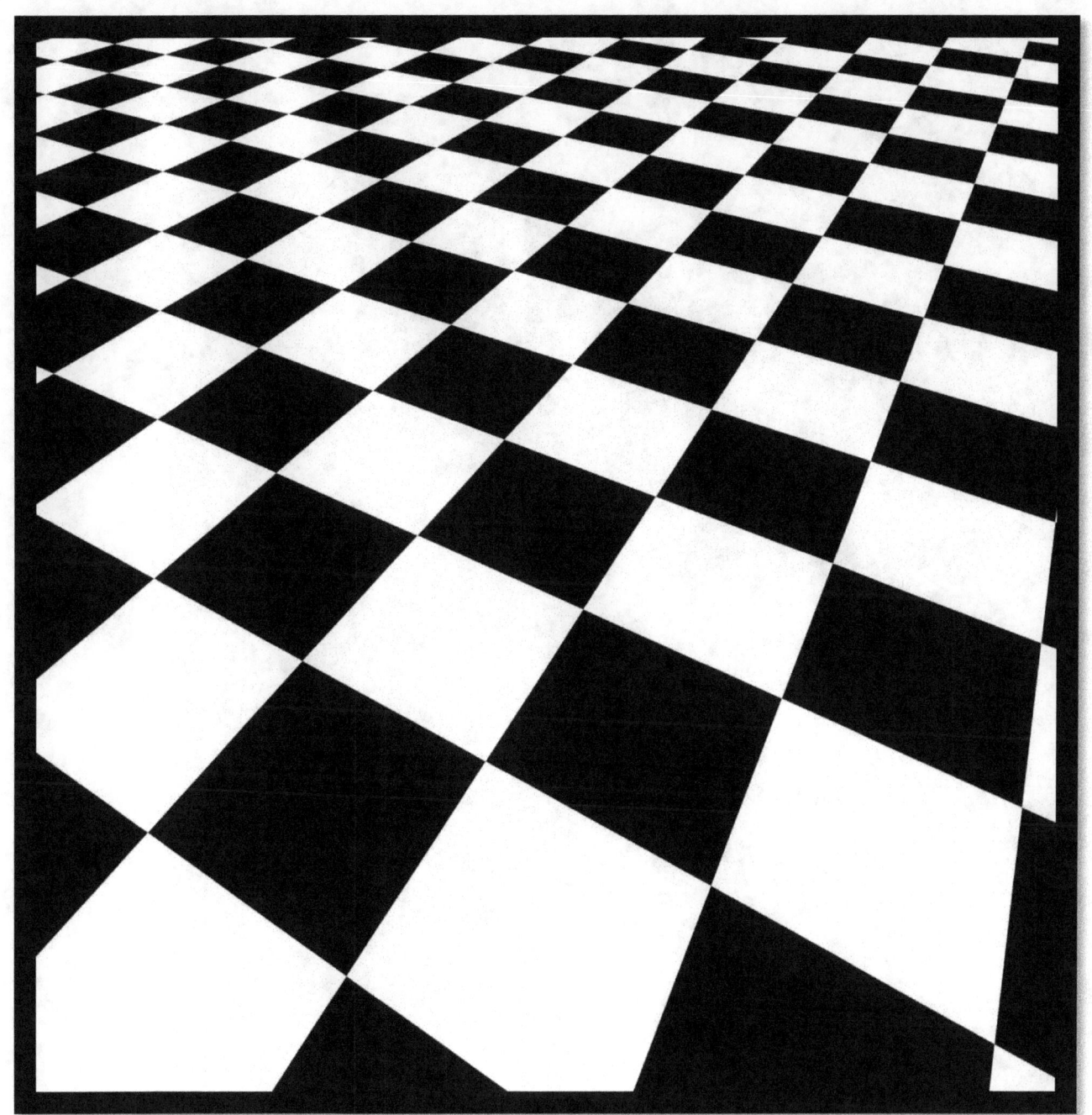

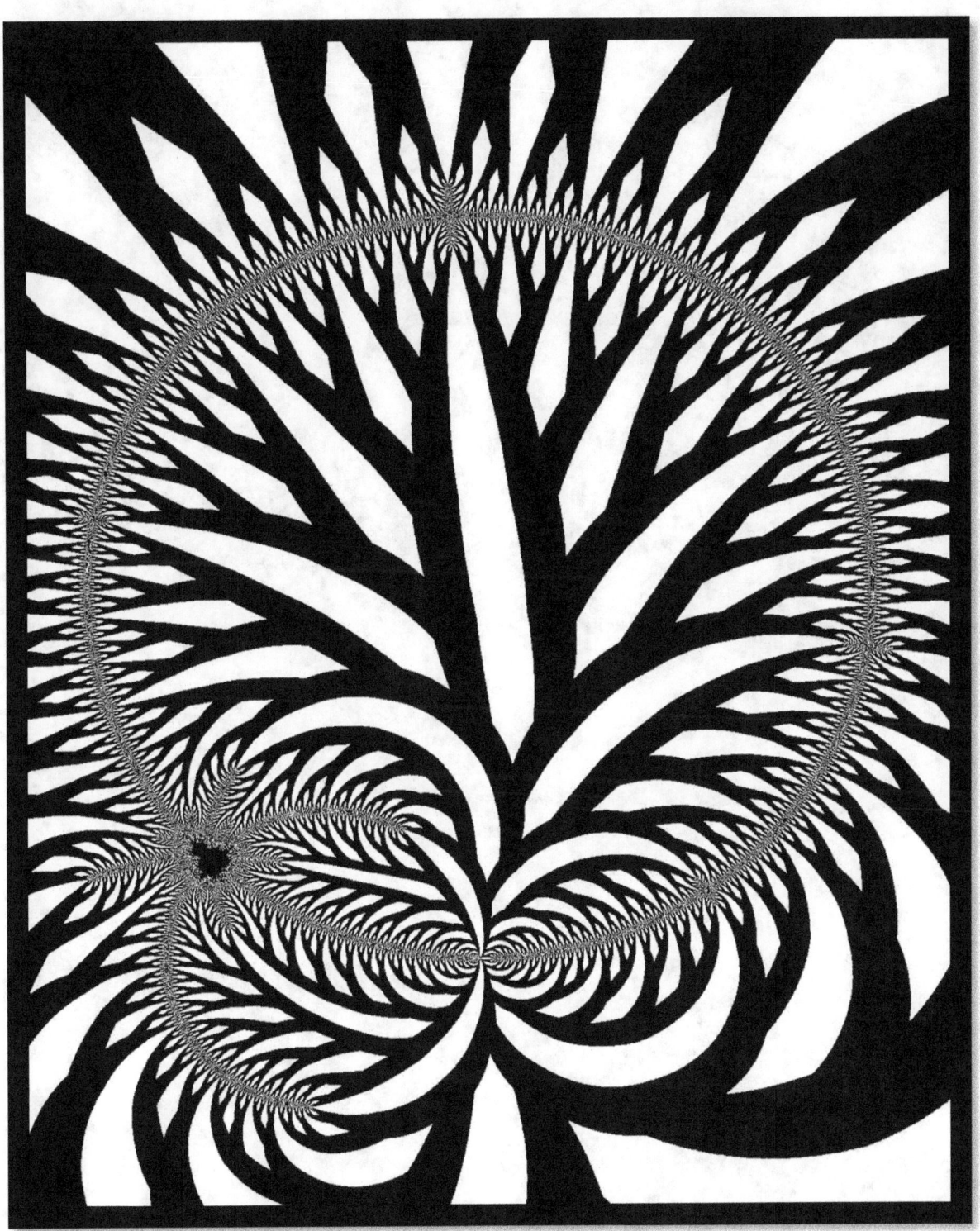

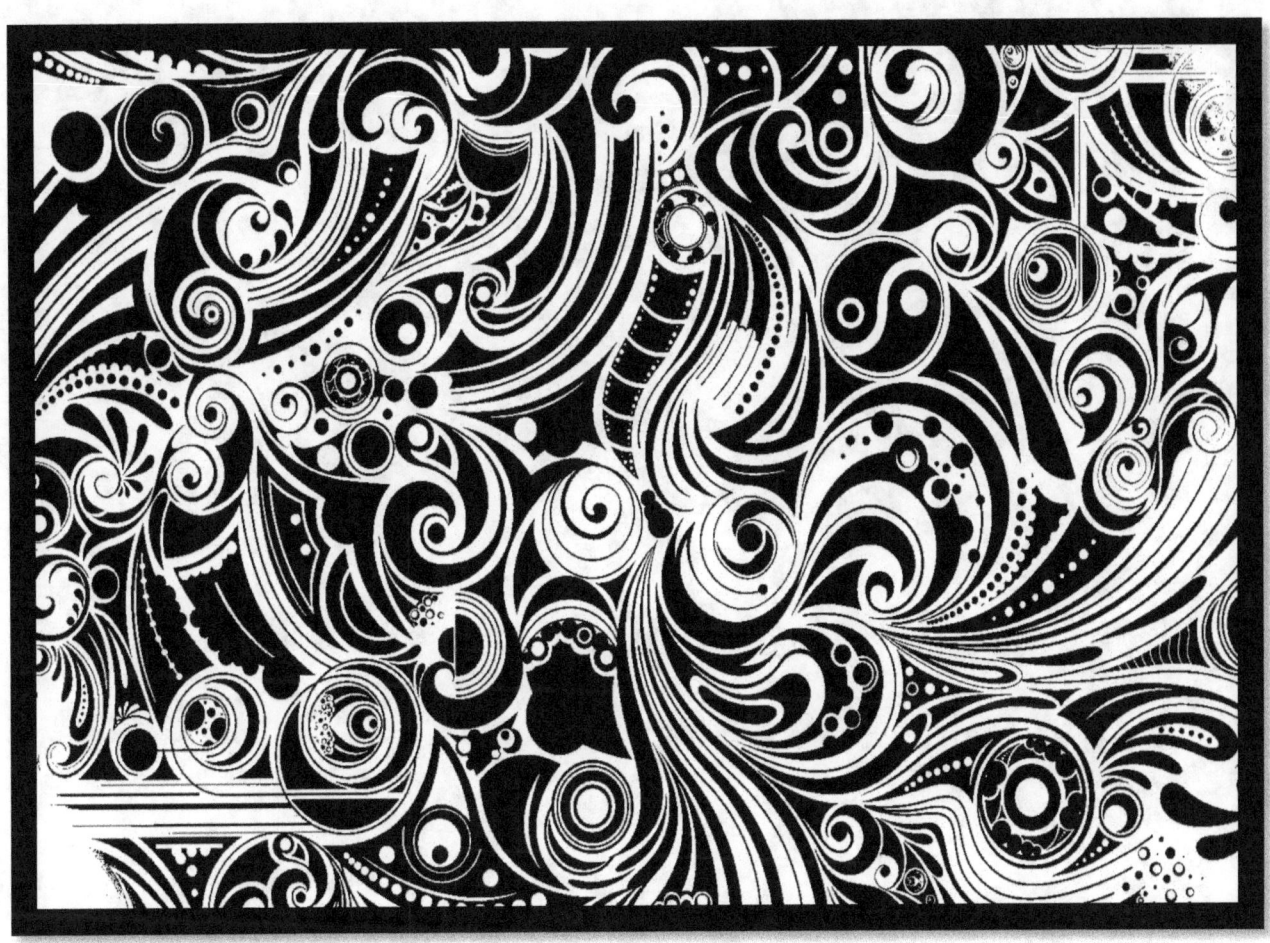

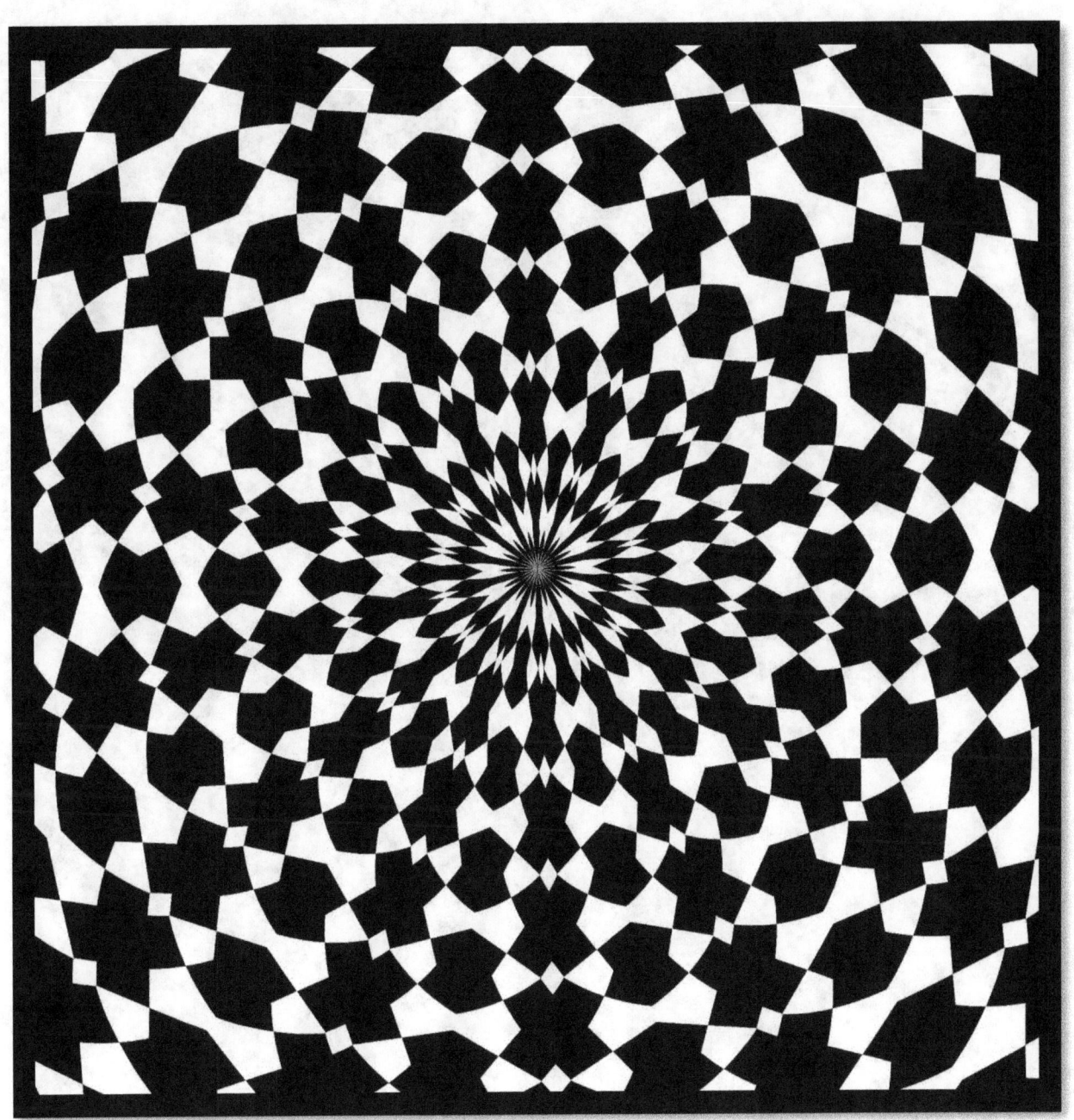

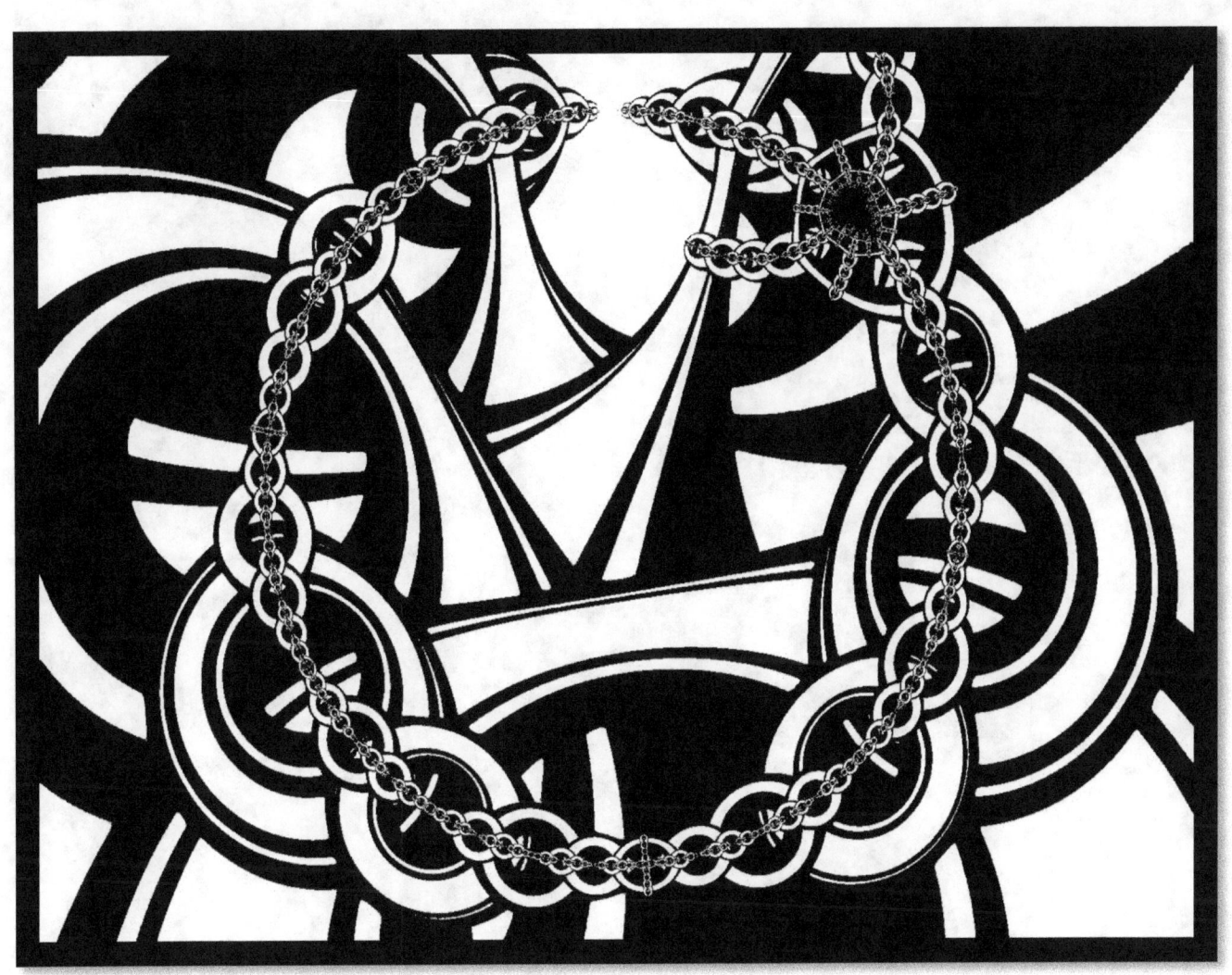

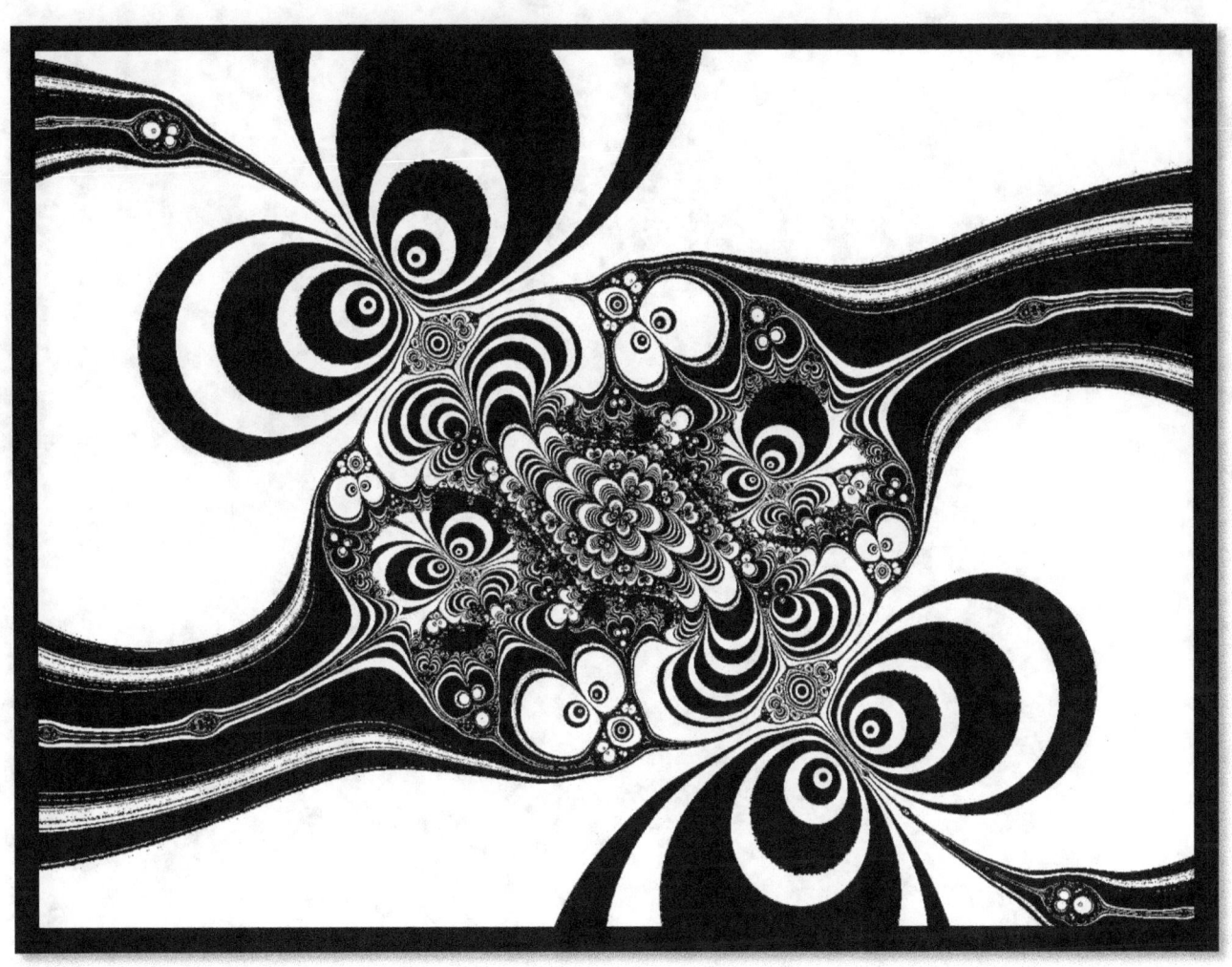

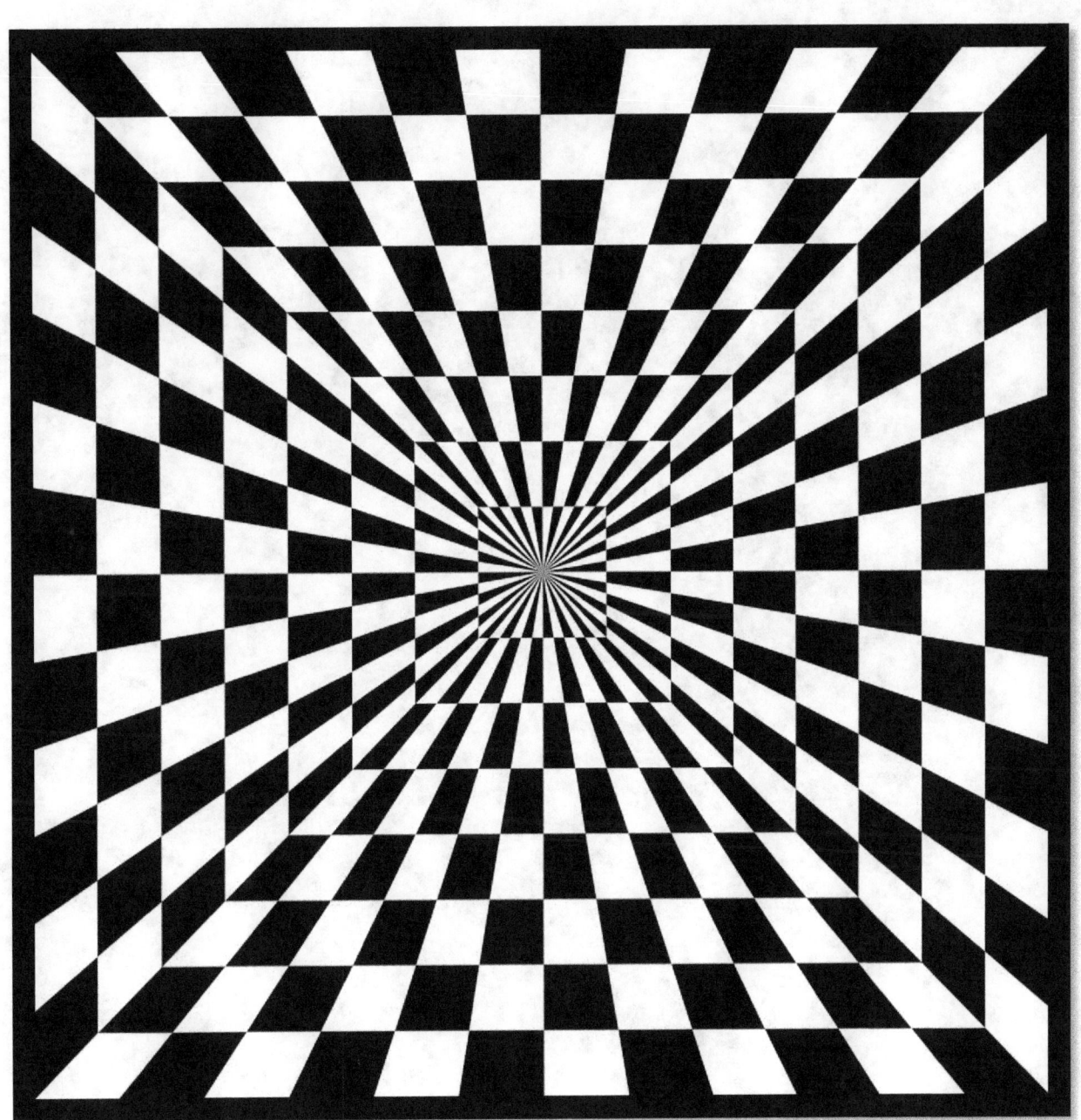

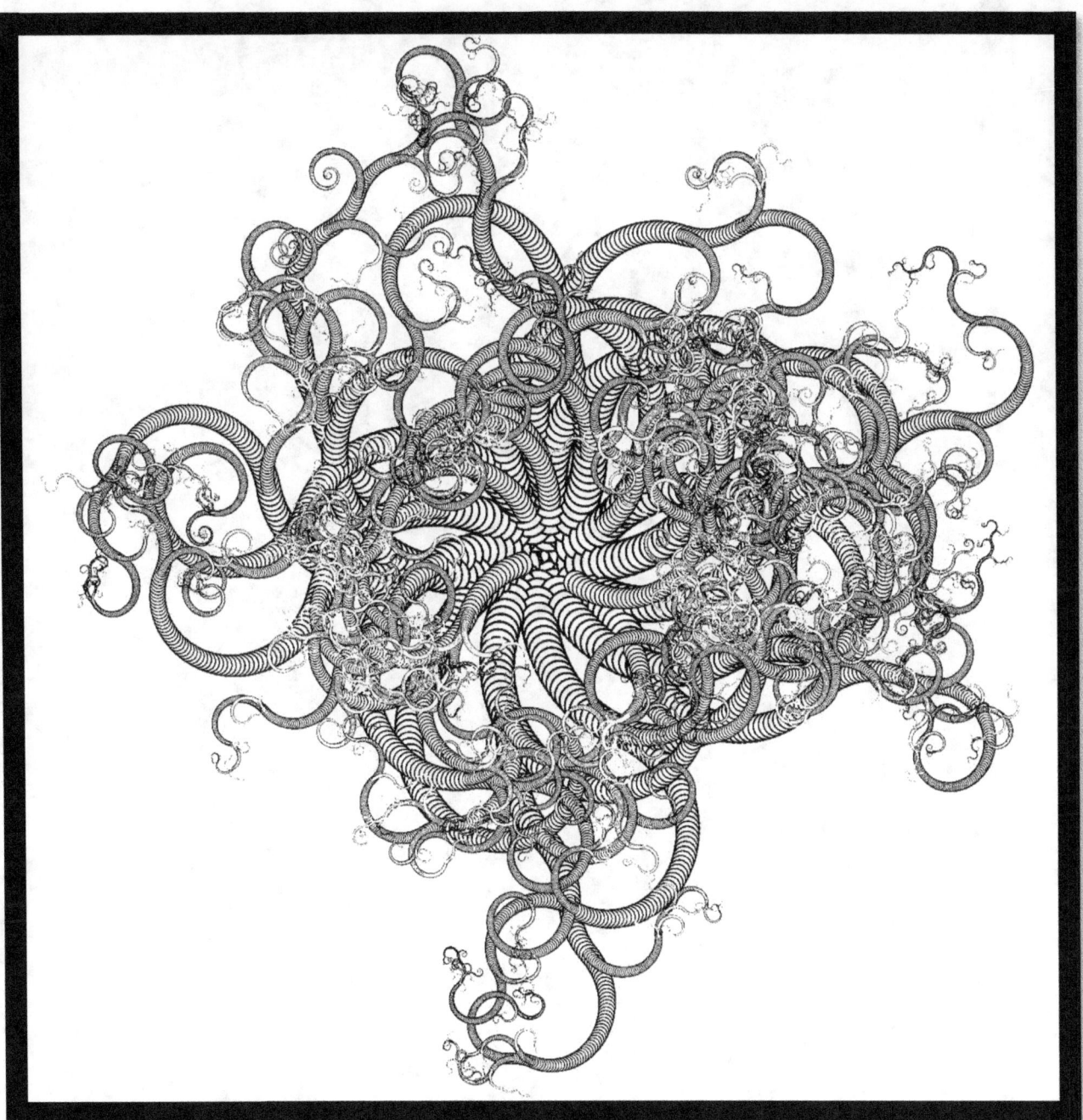

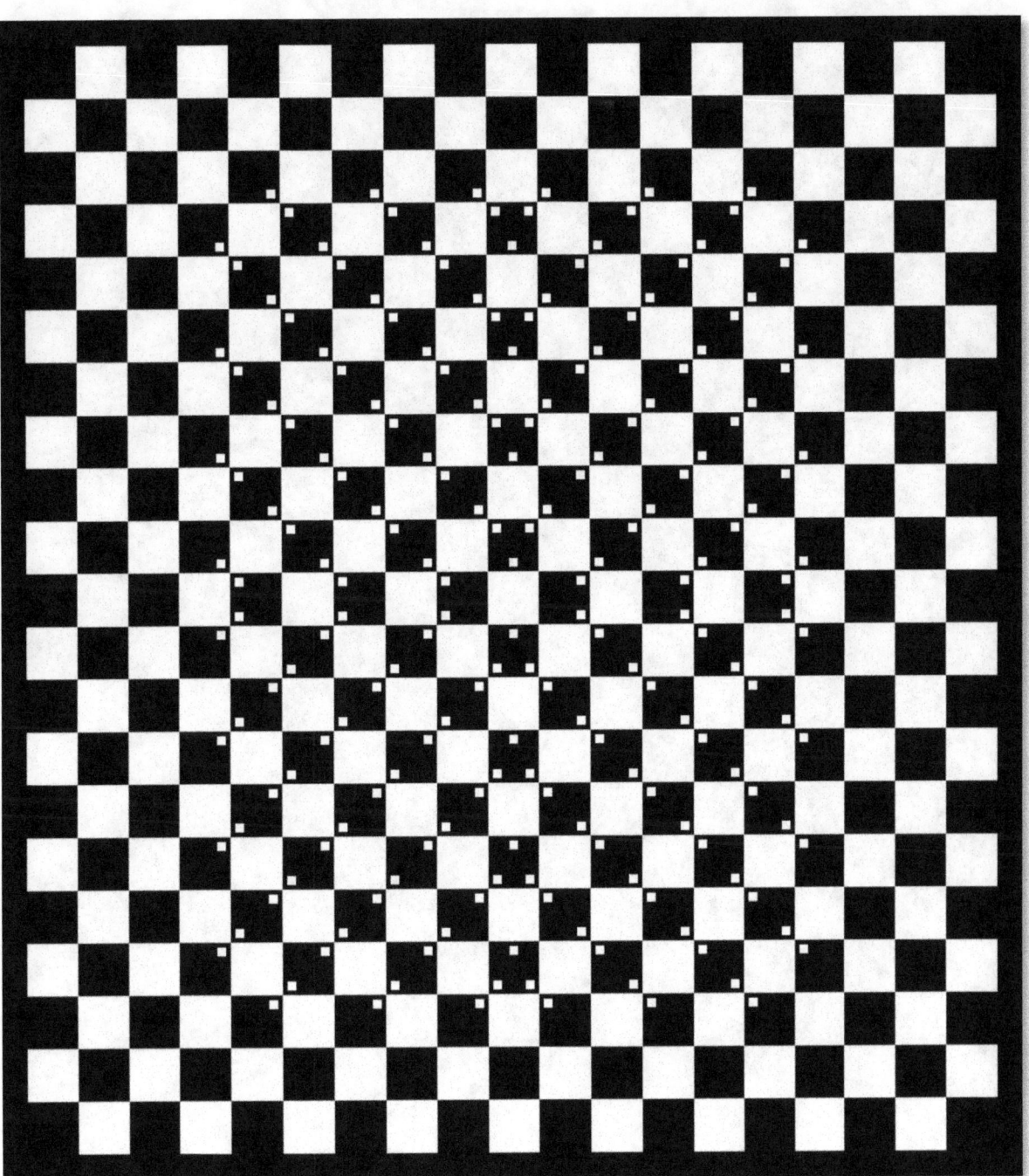

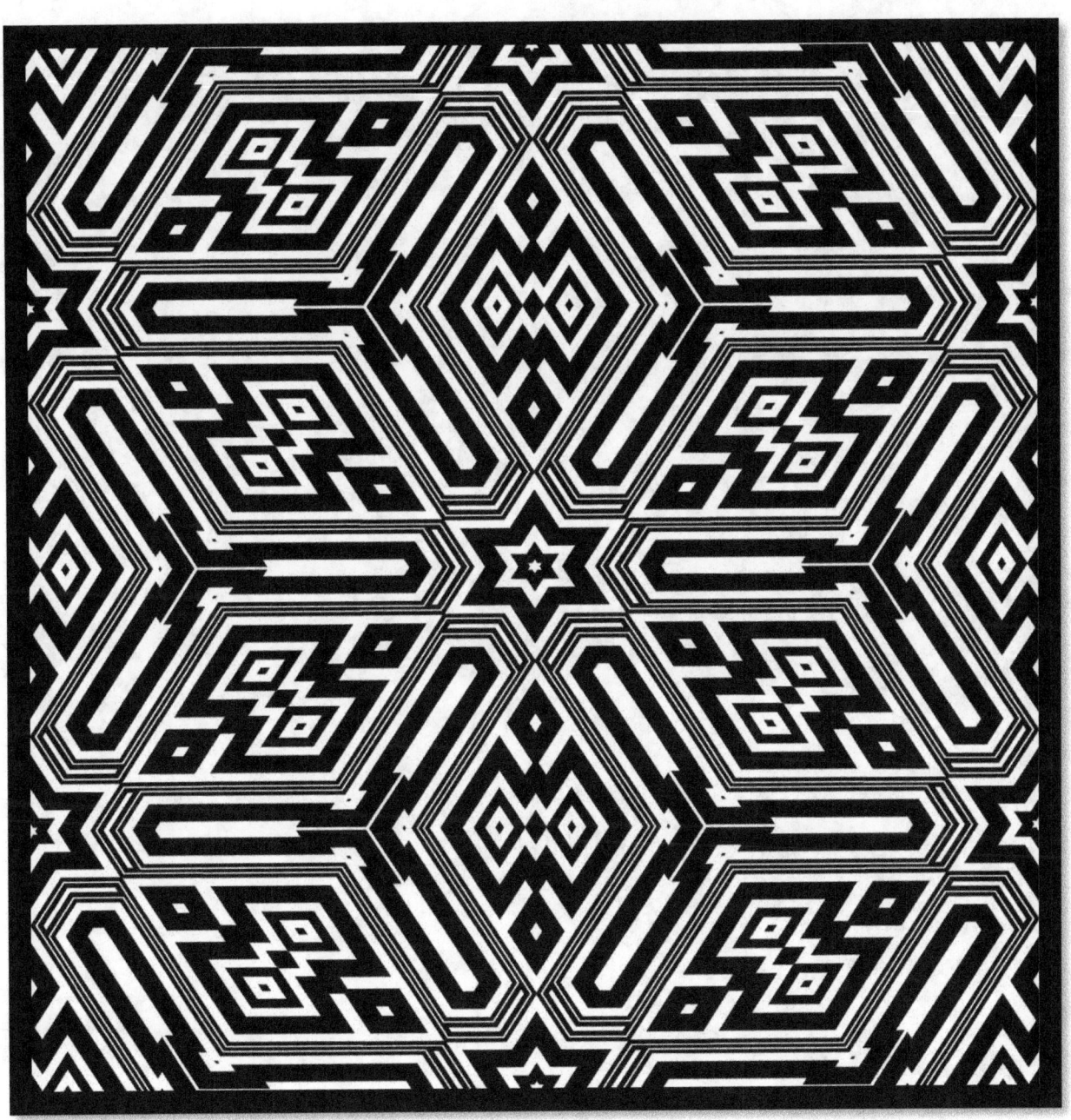

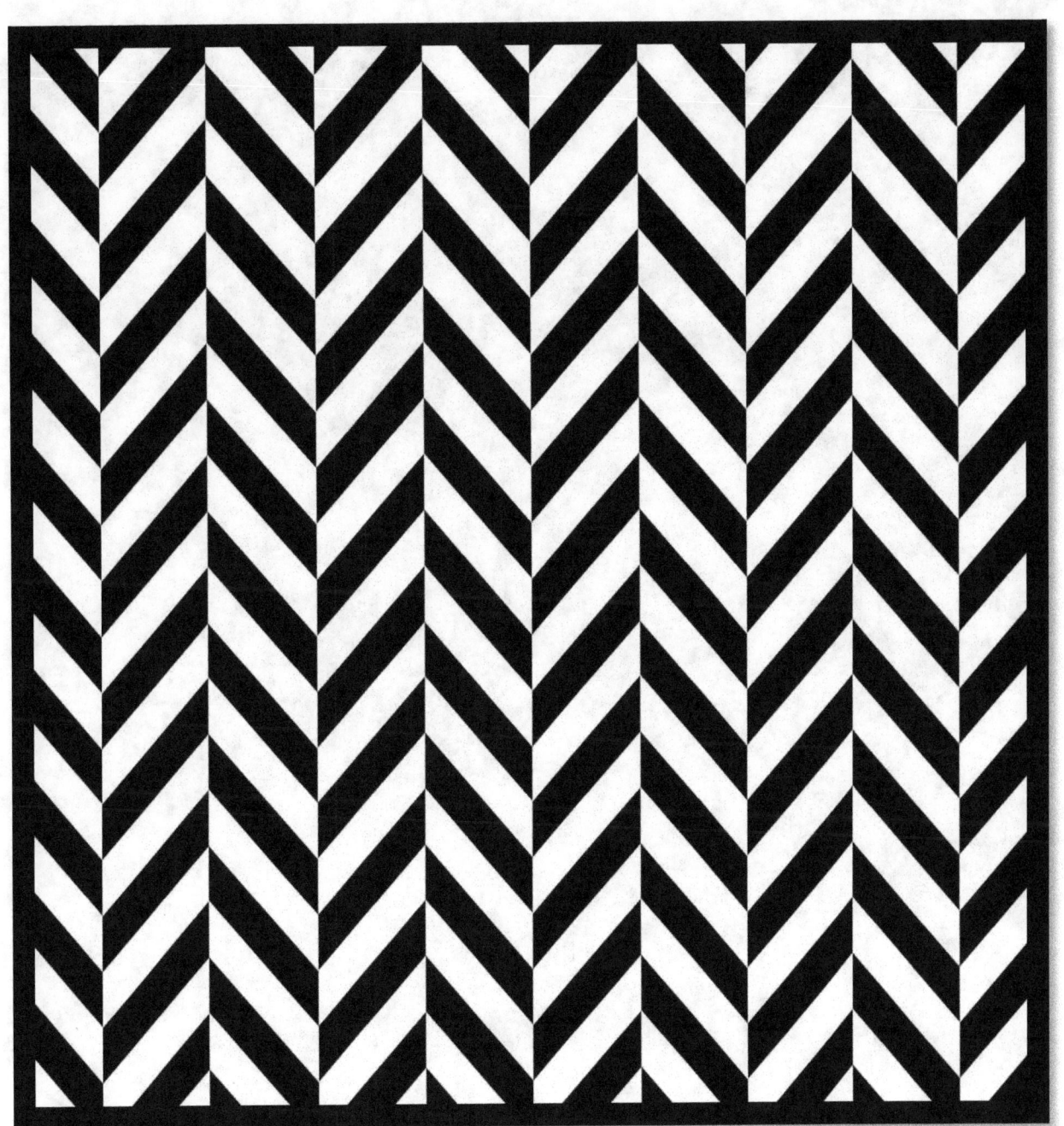

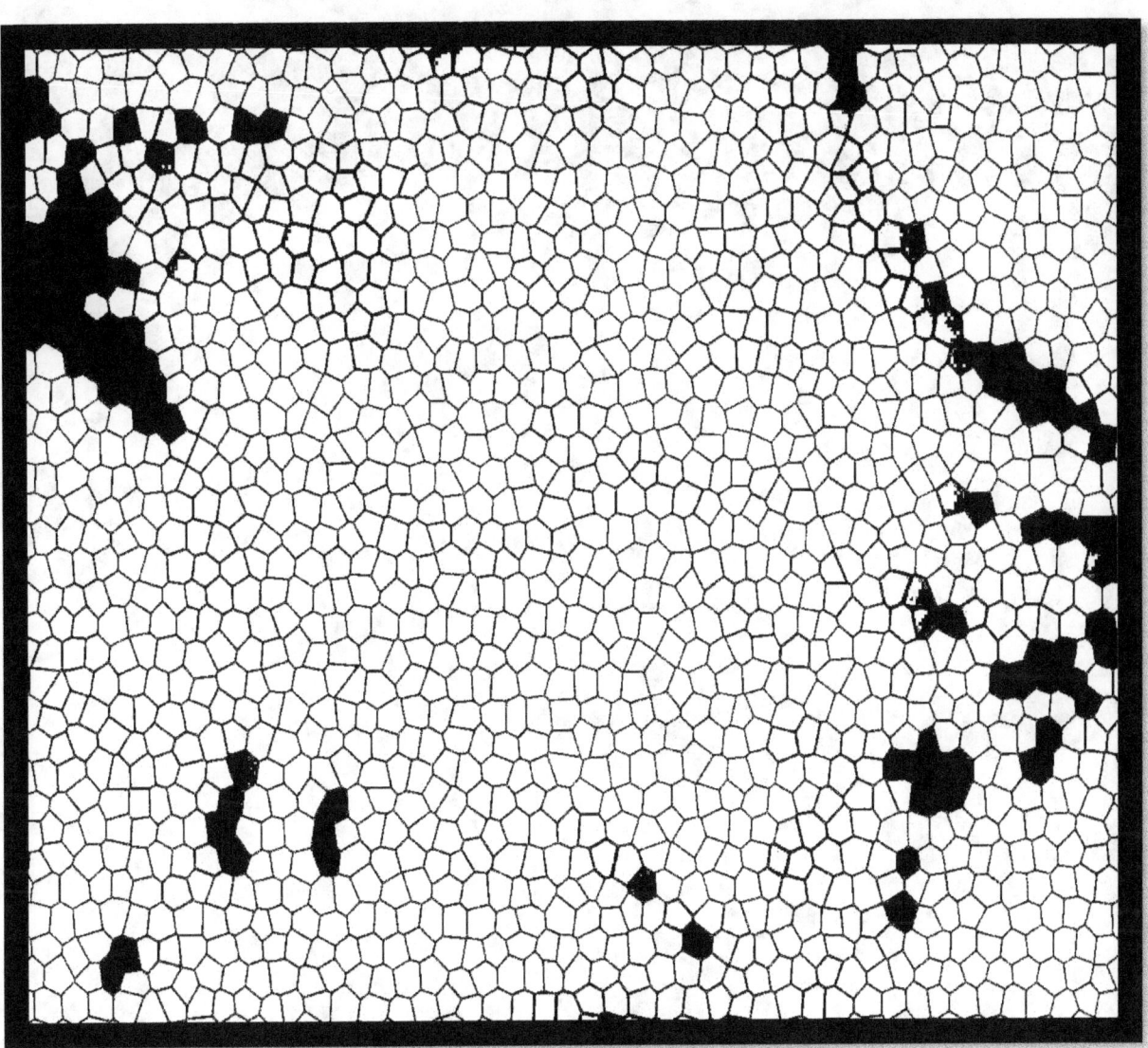

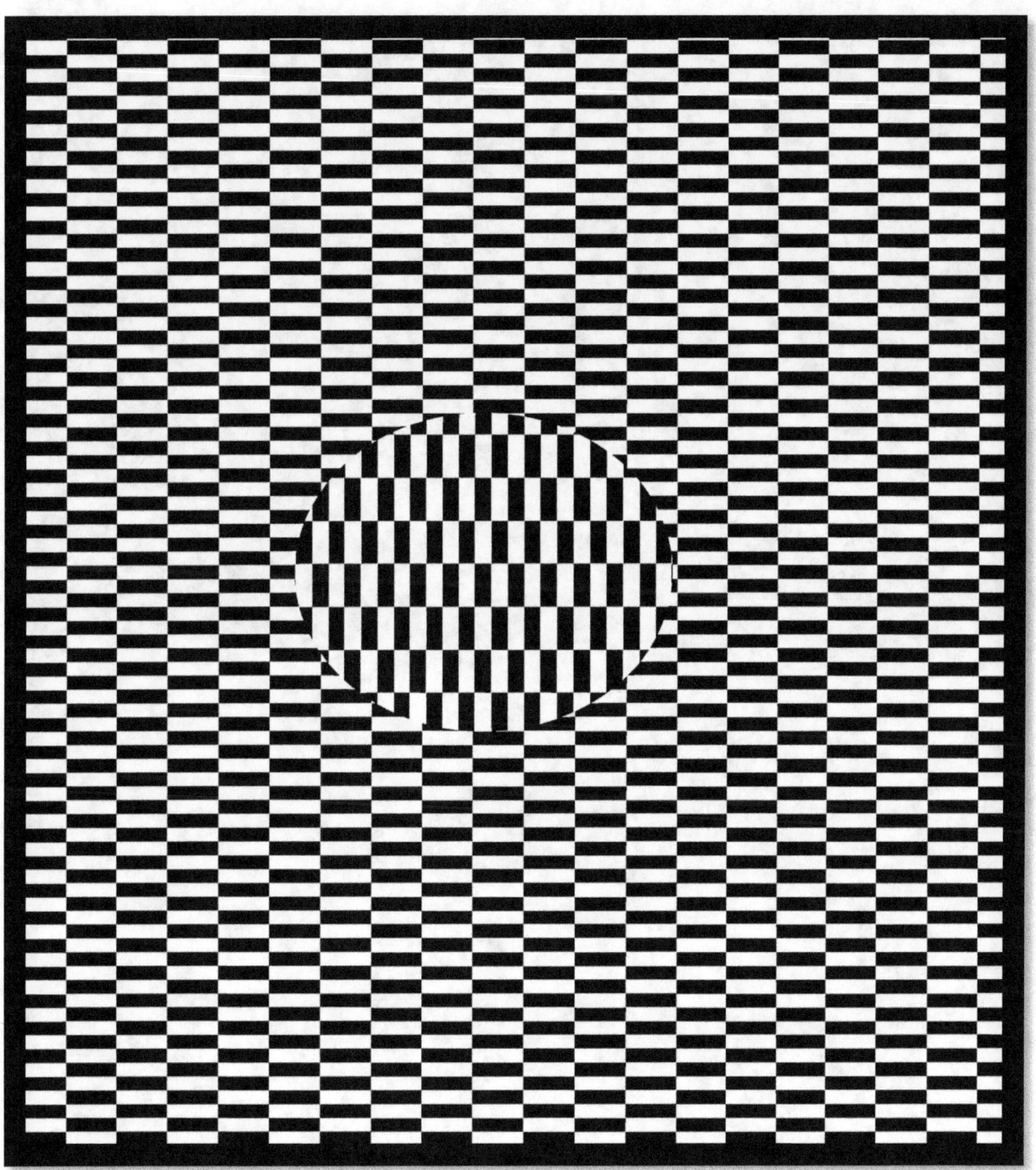

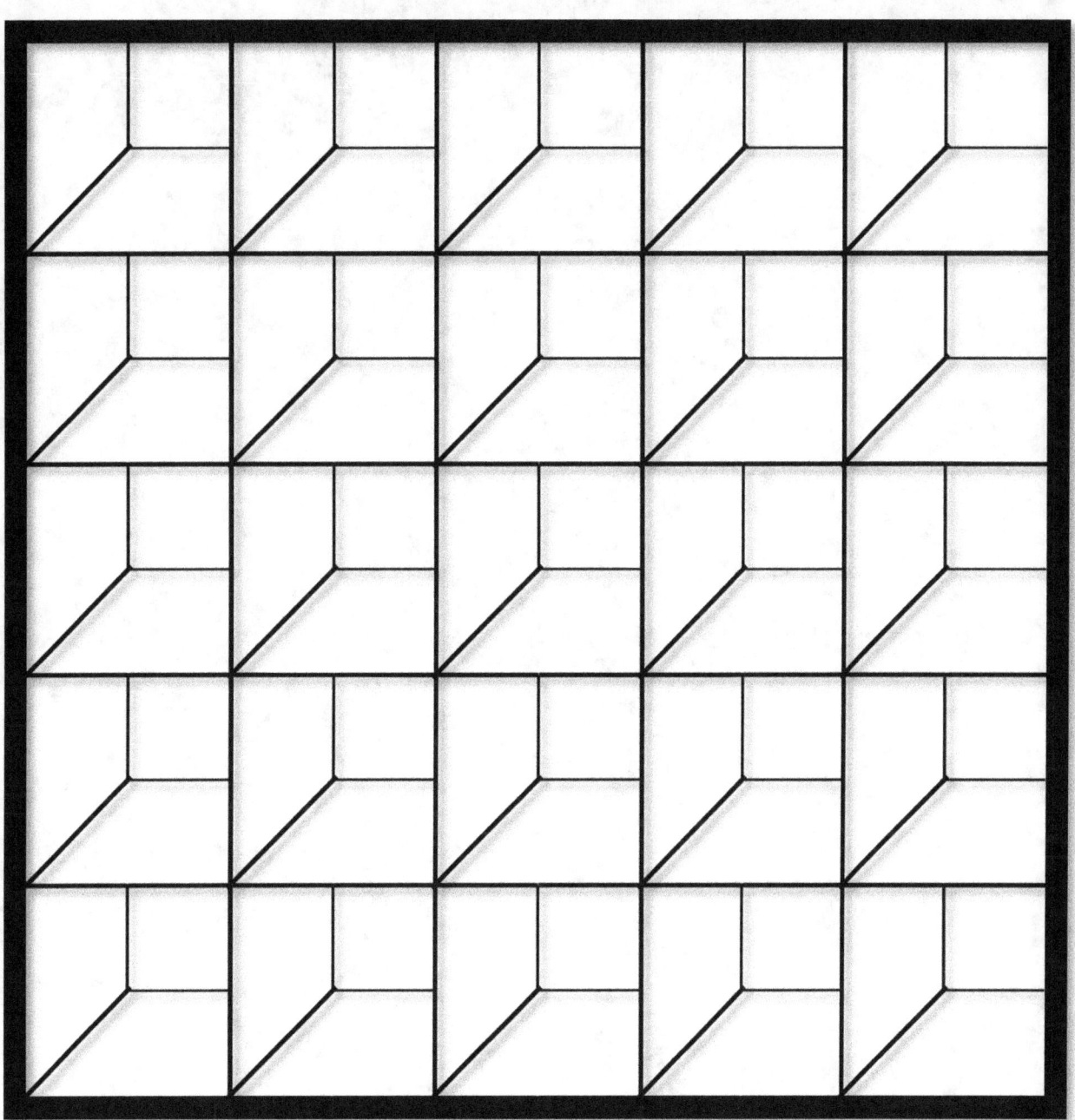

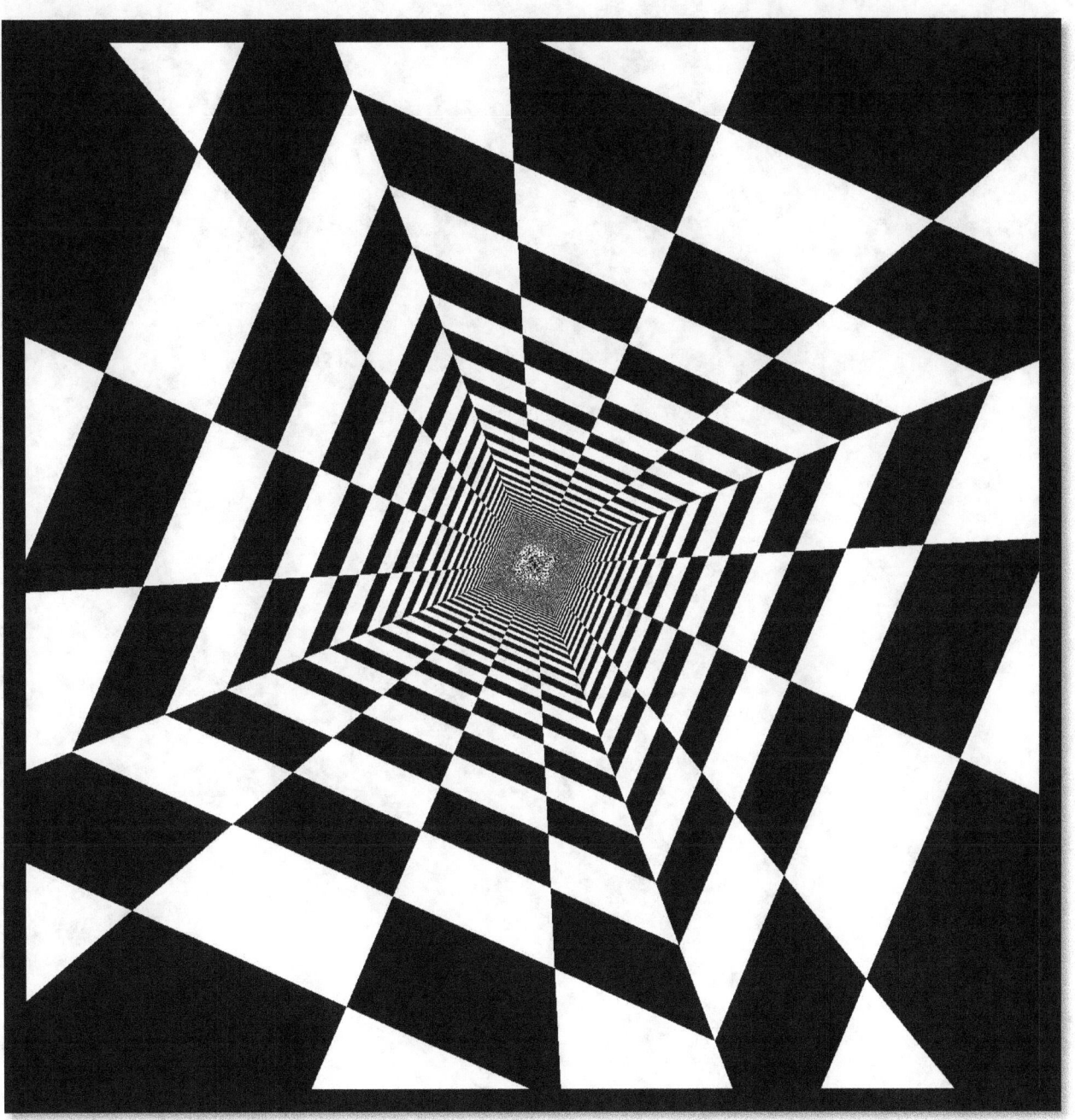

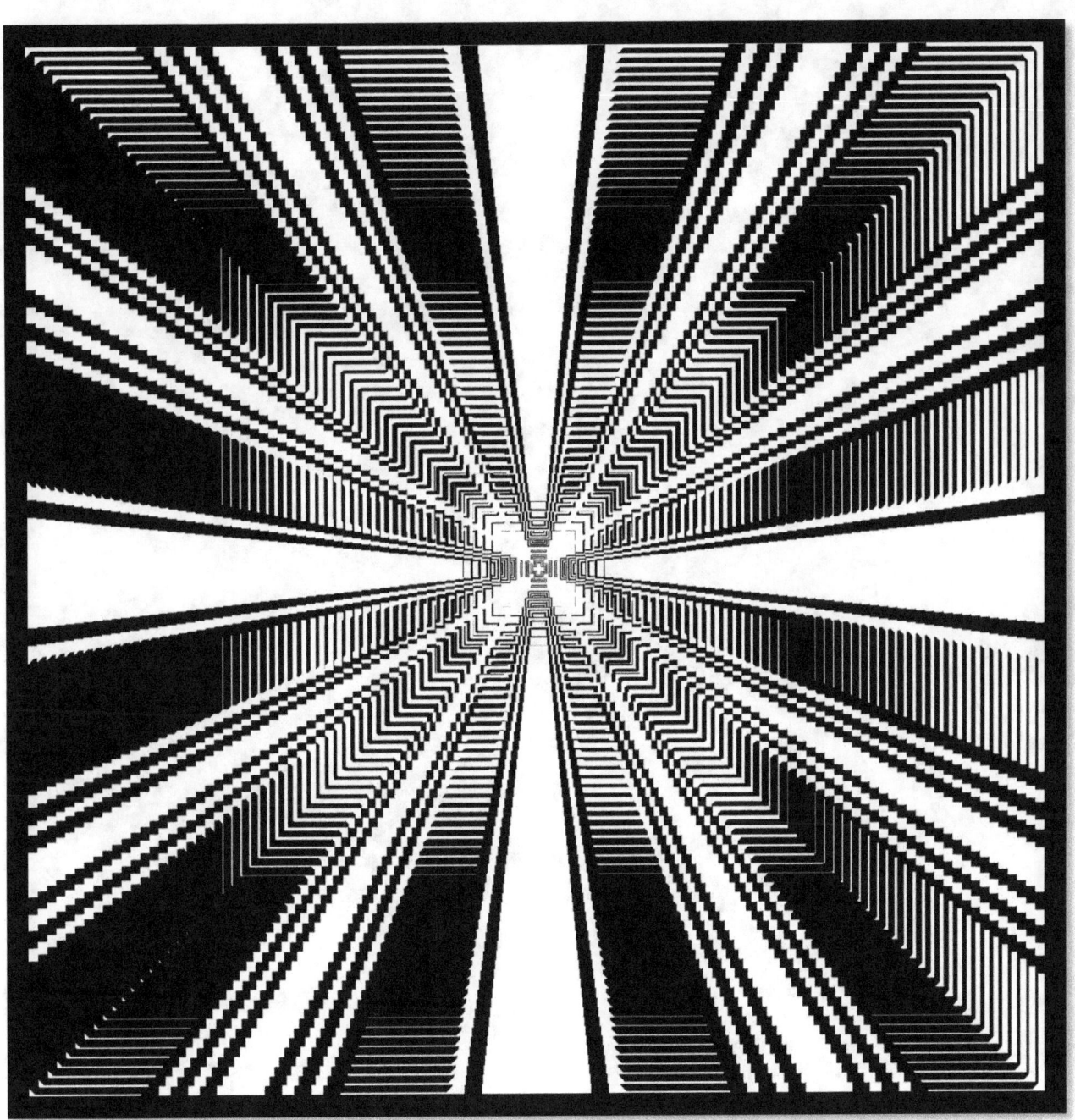

www.ingramcontent.com/pod-product-compliance
Lightning Source LLC
Chambersburg PA
CBHW081311180526
45170CB00007B/2652